God's Special Baby

By Joyce Schilder
Illustrated by Kathy Mitter

CONCORDIA®

Publishing House
St. Louis

Dear Parents:
On each page of this book is a window that con-
tains a symbol relating to the text on that page.
An explanation of these symbols appears at the
back of this book. Older children will enjoy this
added feature as you read this book to your
young child.

The Editor

Copyright © 1984 Concordia Publishing House
3558 S. Jefferson Avenue, St. Louis, MO 63118
Manufactured in the United States of America

Library of Congress Cataloging-in-Publication Data
Schilder, Joyce, 1952-
    God's special baby.
    (God's little learner series)
    Summary: Presents major Biblical characters as babies, leading up to Jesus, God's most special
baby.
    1. Infants in the Bible—Biography—Juvenile literature. 2. Jesus Christ—Nativity—Juvenile
literature. 3. Bible—Biography—Juvenile literature. [1. Children in the Bible. 2. Jesus Christ—
Nativity. 3. Bible stories] I. Mitter, Kathy, ill.
II. Title. III. Series.
BS576.S36   1985   220.9'505   85-17414
ISBN 0-570-04088-4

1   2   3   4   5   6   7   8   9   10   DB   93   92   91   90   89   87   86   85   84

Before the world began
there was nothing but God.

Then God created everything there is.
He made a man and a woman to be His friends.
God called them Adam and Eve.

Although Adam and Eve were happy
in the garden God gave them,
they disobeyed God.
Now they felt bad.
But God promised Adam and Eve that one day
He would make things right again.
He would give the world a special baby—
His own Son.

In time God gave to Adam and Eve a baby.
They called him Cain.
And then they had another baby.
They called him Abel.

And many, many babies were born.
One baby was named Isaac.
His father and mother were called
Abraham and Sarah.
Was this the special baby God had promised?

Years later another baby was born.
His name was Joseph.
His father and mother were called
Jacob and Rachel.
Was this the special baby God had promised?

Many years later a baby boy was born whose name was Moses.
He became a great leader of his people.
Was this God's special baby?

One day a woman named Hannah prayed
and prayed for a baby.
She gave birth to a son
and called him Samuel.
Was this the baby God had promised?

The people waited and waited
for God's special baby.
One day a baby was born whose name
was David.
The people made him a king and
said he was the most special of all.
But was this God's special baby?

Finally one day God sent a message
to a young woman named Mary.
"It is time for My special baby to be born."

God made His special baby and
gave Him to the world—
a baby called Jesus.
"He is My Son, My only Son," said God,
"and He shall make things right."

 This picture reminds us of how Adam and Eve disobeyed God. Do you remember the story about how the sneaky snake tricked Eve? She ate the fruit, and Adam did too!

 God gave Adam and Eve two sons, Cain and Abel. This picture shows what the two sons did. Cain was a farmer, and Abel took care of the sheep.

 One night God made Abraham a big promise. God said that Abraham would have as many children as the stars in the sky. How many stars can you count?

 Jacob and Rachel loved their son Joseph. One day Jacob gave Joseph a long, pretty coat. Was Joseph the special baby God promised would make things right?

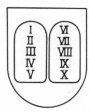 Moses was the great leader of God's people. God gave him special jobs to do. One of these was to give the people the Ten Commandments. Can you say one of them?

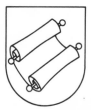 God said yes to Hannah's prayer, and Samuel was born. She was so happy that she thanked God in a special way. She brought Samuel to the temple to serve God there all his life. Can you think of ways to serve God?

 When King David was a boy he liked to play music. This is a picture of what he might have used to play music. He played music to praise God. How can you praise God?

 John the Baptizer got the people ready for God's special baby. He baptized people in the water of a stream and told them about God's special baby.

 Finally God gave His special baby to the world. The baby was named Jesus. He was born in a manger—a bed of straw. God put a big, beautiful star in the sky to tell the world that His special baby had come.

 God's promise of a special baby was for all people. The baby Jesus came "to make things right." He did that on the cross. He died for your sins and for everybody's sins. Can you tell your friends about God's special baby and how He made things right?